Yellow Umbrella Books are published by Capstone Press
151 Good Counsel Drive, P.O. Box 669, Mankato, Minnesota 56002
www.capstonepress.com

Library of Congress Cataloging-in-Publication Data
Catala, Ellen.
  Our five senses / by Ellen Catala.
    p. cm.—(Science)
    Includes Index.
Summary: Presents a brief statement of the role of each of the five senses.
"Yellow Umbrella Books."
Includes index.
  ISBN-13: 978-0-7368-2021-9 (hardcover)
  ISBN-10: 0-7368-2021-3 (hardcover)
  1. Senses and sensation–Juvenile literature. [1. Senses and sensation.] I. Title. II. Science (Mankato, Minn.)
  QP434.C383 2003
  612.8–dc21

                                                                      2003000936

Editorial Credits
Mary Lindeen, Editorial Director; Jennifer Van Voorst, Editor; Wanda Winch, Photo Researcher

Photo Credits
Cover: Erin Hogan/PhotoDisc; Title Page: Photo 24/Brand X Pictures; Page 2: Keith Brofsky/PhotoDisc; Page 3: Comstock; Page 4: Gerry Ellis and Michael Durham/Digital Vision; Page 5: Comstock; Page 6: PhotoLink/PhotoDisc; Page 7: Ron Chapple/Thinkstock; Page 8: Comstock; Page 9: Mark Andersen/RubberBall Productions; Page 10: Ron Chapple/Thinkstock; Page 11: Mark Andersen/RubberBall Productions; Page 12: Mark Andersen/RubberBall Productions; Page 13: Mark Andersen/RubberBall Productions; Page 14: Rob Van Petten/Digital Vision; Page 15: Rob Van Petten/Digital Vision; Page 16: Corbis

Our Five Senses

by Ellen Catala

Consultant: Eric H. Chudler, Ph.D., Research Associate Professor, Department of Anesthesiology, University of Washington, Seattle

Yellow Umbrella Books

an imprint of Capstone Press
Mankato, Minnesota

How do we learn about our world?

We use our five senses.

We use our eyes
to see things.

We learn how things look.

We use our ears to hear things.

We learn how things sound.

We use our noses to smell things.

We learn how things smell.

We use our fingers to touch things.

We learn how things feel.

We use our mouths to taste things.

We learn how things taste.

Most of the time we use all five senses at once!

Our five senses help us learn about our world.

How have you used your senses today?

Words to Know/Index

feel—to touch something with your fingers, or to experience something touching you; page 11

hear—to sense sounds through your ears; page 6

see—to use your eyes, to look at or notice something or someone; page 4

senses— the powers a living being uses to learn about its surroundings; pages 3, 14, 15, 16

smell—to sense an odor with your nose; pages 8, 9

sound—a noise that you can hear; page 7

taste—a sense allowing you to identify food by its flavor; pages 12, 13

touch—to make contact with your hand or another area of your body; page 10

Word Count: 99
Early-Intervention Level: 7